FORCE RECON

BY CHARLES MARLIN

WWW.APEXEDITIONS.COM

Apex is distributed by North Star Editions:
sales@northstareditions.com | 888-417-0195

Produced for Apex by Red Line Editorial.

Photographs ©: Sgt. Daisha R. Ramirez/US Marine Corps/DVIDS, cover; Lance Cpl. Malik Lewis/US Marine Corps/DVIDS, 1, 24–25; Petty Officer 2nd Class William Farmerie/US Navy/DVIDS, 4–5, 6; Petty Officer 1st Class David McKee/US Navy/DVIDS, 7, 29; Cmdr. Christopher Nodine/US Navy/DVIDS, 9; Hulton Archive/Archive Photos/Getty Images, 10–11; Lance Cpl. Emma Gray/US Marine Corps/DVIDS, 12–13, 26; Cpl. Andre Dakis/US Marine Corps/DVIDS, 14; Cpl. Breanna L. Weisenberger/US Marine Corps/DVIDS, 16–17, 18–19; Pfc. Kaleb Martin/US Marine Corps/DVIDS, 18; Lance Cpl. Audrey M. C. Rampton/US Marine Corps/DVIDS, 20–21; Cpl. Angel Diaz Montes De Oca/US Marine Corps/DVIDS, 22–23; Petty Officer 1st Class Almagissel Schuring/US Navy/DVIDS, 27

Library of Congress Control Number: 2025939208

ISBN
979-8-89250-805-6 (hardcover)
979-8-89250-834-6 (paperback)
979-8-89250-889-6 (ebook pdf)
979-8-89250-863-6 (hosted ebook)

Printed in the United States of America
Mankato, MN
012026

NOTE TO PARENTS AND EDUCATORS

Apex books are designed to build literacy skills in striving readers. Exciting, high-interest content attracts and holds readers' attention. The text is carefully leveled to allow students to achieve success quickly. Additional features, such as bolded glossary words for difficult terms, help build comprehension.

TABLE OF CONTENTS

CHAPTER 1

STOPPING PIRATES

In September 2010, pirates took over a **cargo ship**. US Marines sped to the scene on a big ship. A Force Recon team was on board.

The USS *Dubuque* (left) came to help when pirates captured a cargo ship (right) near Yemen.

Marine Corps helicopters helped distract the pirates.

Some US Marines caught the pirates' attention. Meanwhile, Force Recon **launched** small boats. They sneaked closer. Then the team climbed onto the cargo ship.

FAST FACT

Force Recon teams often ride **inflatable** boats to reach targets.

Two small boats brought the Force Recon team toward the cargo ship.

The pirates were shocked. Some tried to run. Others surrendered without a fight. Force Recon caught them all.

SAVING THE CREW

When Force Recon arrived, the ship's crew was hiding. They had locked themselves in the engine room. Force Recon broke down the doors. The team rescued all 11 crew members.

Force Recon saved the cargo ship without firing a single shot.

MAGELLAN STAR
ST. JOHN'S

CHAPTER 2

FORCE RECON HISTORY

Force Recon is part of the US Marine Corps. In World War II (1939–1945), the Marine Corps formed new groups. They worked on both water and land.

During World War II, teams of US Marines helped attack islands in the Pacific Ocean.

Later, those groups became known as Force Recon. In the 1990s and 2000s, Force Recon often worked in the Middle East. For example, some of the teams fought near the Persian Gulf.

Force Recon teams often use ropes and helicopters to quickly drop soldiers into enemy areas.

Today, Force Recon carries out missions around the world. Teams go deep into enemy territory. Some teams spy. Others do surprise attacks.

GREEN AND BLACK

Force Recon does two main types of missions. Some missions involve gathering information. These are called "green operations." Other missions are attacks. They're known as "black operations."

Force Recon Marines sometimes parachute down to their targets.

CHAPTER 3

TOUGH TRAINING

To join Force Recon, people must first become Marines. Then, they must pass difficult tests. The tests show their fitness on land and in water.

To pass Force Recon tests, people must be fast and strong. Many Marines fail or need several tries.

Force Recon Marines must be able to carry a gun while treading water.

During testing, Marines swim deep underwater. They race through **obstacle courses**. They also run and tread water.

One test has Marines run several miles while carrying heavy packs.

Some Force Recon Marines get extra training in shooting rifles.

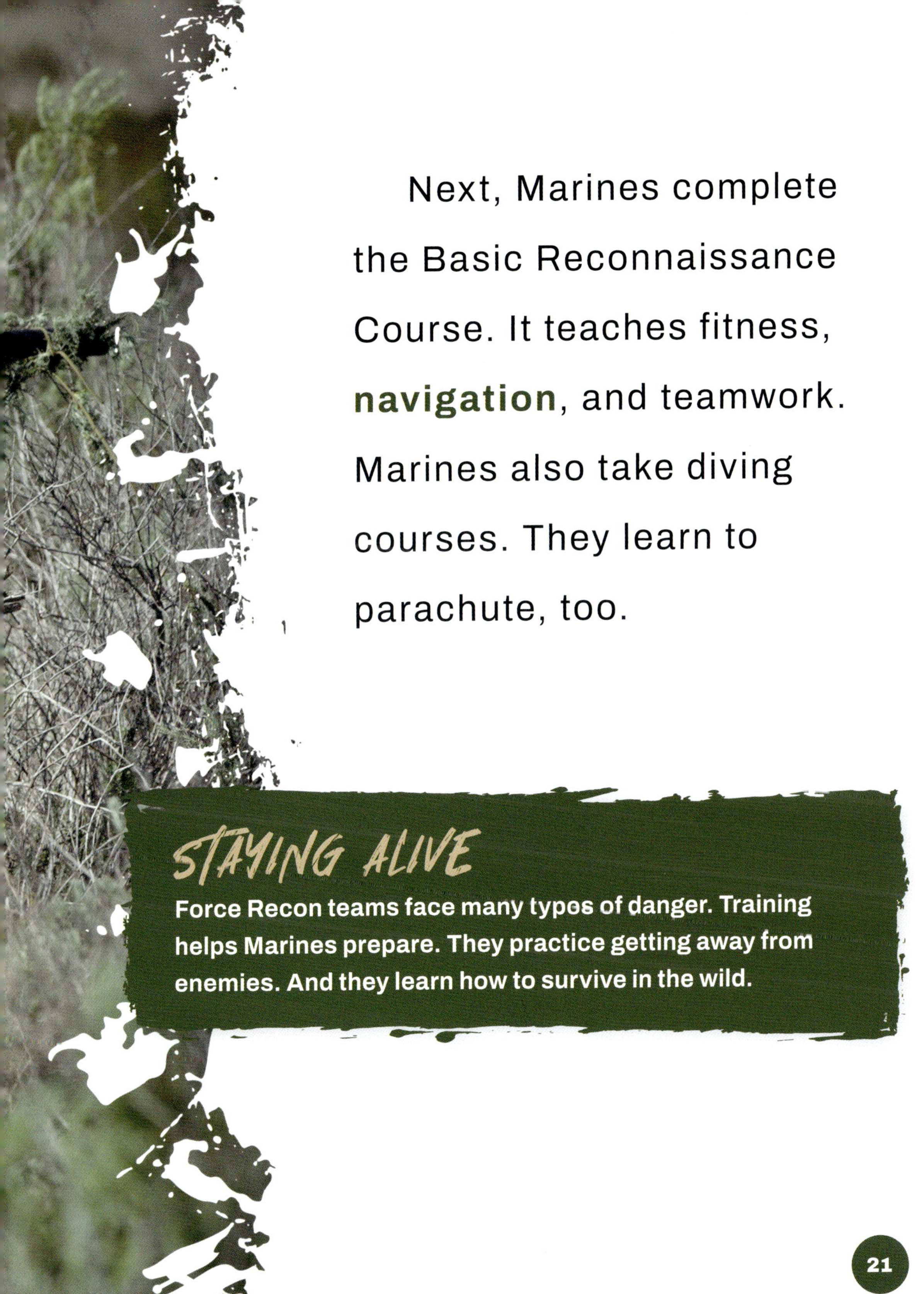

Next, Marines complete the Basic Reconnaissance Course. It teaches fitness, **navigation**, and teamwork. Marines also take diving courses. They learn to parachute, too.

STAYING ALIVE

Force Recon teams face many types of danger. Training helps Marines prepare. They practice getting away from enemies. And they learn how to survive in the wild.

CHAPTER 4

ON A MISSION

Force Recon teams usually have six people. Several teams form a bigger group called a platoon. And several platoons make up a company.

During many missions, a Force Recon platoon works alongside other Marines.

Each team uses high-tech equipment. Marines often carry radios and night vision goggles.

Pistols and rifles are common weapons. Teams may also fire **grenades** or rockets.

Force Recon teams may use M203 grenade launchers. They can shoot grenades nearly 1,150 feet (350 m).

FAST FACT

The Force Recon **motto** is "swift, silent, deadly."

For some missions, teams ride in **submarines**. While on the surface, Marines may launch boats from subs. Or Marines may swim out while subs are underwater.

Force Recon teams can launch a boat from a submarine in less than two minutes.

Force Recon Marines swim around a submarine in the Mediterranean Sea.

DIVING

Force Recon Marines often **scuba dive**. They may secretly swim toward enemy land. Or they may record details about enemy areas. For example, they may study the shape of the shore.

COMPREHENSION QUESTIONS

Write your answers on a separate piece of paper.

1. Write a few sentences explaining the two types of missions Force Recon teams do.

2. Which type of test described in Chapter 2 seems hardest to you? Why?

3. How many people are usually part of a Force Recon team?

   A. six people
   B. nine people
   C. 11 people

4. Why might Force Recon teams study the shape of an enemy's shore?

   A. so they could help that enemy
   B. so they could plan an attack
   C. so they could not be sneaky

5. What does **surrendered** mean in this book?

*The pirates were shocked. Some tried to run. Others **surrendered** without a fight. Force Recon caught them all.*

A. won a fight
B. got away
C. gave up

6. What does **equipment** mean in this book?

*Each team uses high-tech **equipment**. Marines often carry radios and night vision goggles.*

A. food and water
B. gear or tools
C. types of plants

Answer key on page 32.

GLOSSARY

cargo ship

A ship that carries items from one place to another.

grenades

Small bombs that are thrown or launched.

inflatable

Able to be filled with air.

launched

Sent a boat into the water.

motto

A short sentence or phrase that describes a group's beliefs.

navigation

Finding one's location and planning which way to go.

obstacle courses

Paths filled with things that block the way.

scuba dive

To swim while wearing flippers and air tanks, which help people move and breathe underwater.

submarines

Ships that can stay deep underwater for a long time.

BOOKS

Coupé, Jessica. *US Marine Corps*. Apex Editions, 2023.

Marlin, Charles. *Submarines*. Apex Editions, 2025.

Phillips, Howard. *Inside Marine Force Recon*. PowerKids Press, 2022.

ONLINE RESOURCES

Visit **www.apexeditions.com** to find links and resources related to this title.

ABOUT THE AUTHOR

Charles Marlin is an author, editor, and avid cyclist. He lives in rural Iowa.

INDEX

ANSWER KEY:
1. Answers will vary; 2. Answers will vary; 3. A; 4. B; 5. C; 6. B